HOW THE MAFIA SAVED MY LIFE

HOW THE
MAFIA SAVED
MY LIFE

LA'QUE DUREN

This book is dedicated to the memory of my daughter, Shahida Chontel Duren
January 1967 - December 1993

To the young girls and women all over the world. To those who are being exploited and sold against their will and are used until there is no self-worth. To those who have lost the joy of being little girls and were thrust into womanhood before their time.
The sole purpose of bringing this story to light is to empower you, no matter what you go through. While encountering the dark hard places, against impossible odds, and while asking yourself, "Will I live and make it?" or "If this is life, I don't want it," there is light at the end of the tunnel.

Contents

Broken To Wholeness

I am one of four children; I have two sisters and one brother. I remember so much as a little girl. My father did not live with my mother. They were divorced, but he would take me and my sister shopping for school clothes and holidays. One of my happy memories of him was when I was outside playing. I spotted him coming up the street. He always wore a big hat, and he seemed very tall to me.

I was so happy to see him. He always reached in his pocket and gave me 50 cents.

At that time, I could get a big bag of candy for that. One cent could buy three pieces of candy back then.

My mother's second husband worked on the railroad, and my mom and I would take weekend train trips. I did not like him at all. He was a cook for the railroad and consistently had alcohol on his breath.

I was about five years old when he would touch me and make me feel uncomfortable. When he was around, I was afraid to fall asleep, even on the train. When it was time to get off the train, he carried me, and touched me in a bad way.

The night was not my friend, and I did not want to see the sun go down. He would come into my room at night when it was very dark, but I could see his shadow. I would fight sleep. But I often would succumb to exhaustion, and when I did, I was awakened by something hard on my face and lips.

I told my mom I was afraid of the dark, so she put a night light in my room. I hoped that would stop him, but it didn't. I would see his reflection, and this thing that in the eyes of a young girl, looked like an elephant trunk. Once I went to my mother's room and told her I had seen his trunk. She asked, "What? What do you mean?" I innocently answered that he comes into my room at night. She defensively accused me, "You are not telling me the truth."

I left her room thinking, *what if she tells him?* This was a long held silent fear of mine, but when I grew brave enough to tell her, looking for her to protect me, she turned me away.

My mom was so fearful she injected her fears into me. We would go to the beach, and she would warn me, "Don't go too far! There are suck-holes out there." I became terrified of deep water. I was afraid to walk out too far, and it freaked me out by how the sand moved under my feet in the water. I stayed on shore. My mother taught me that the beach was not a safe place. When she washed my hair, she would waterboard me, holding my head under the waterspout, so I choked. She acted like she did not care. It took me a long time before I could hold my face under the water, even when taking a shower.

I played with evil children, who I thought were my friends. They would trick me into going in the closet by saying, "We are going to hide." But they shoved me in the closet and locked the door, so I could not get out. It seemed like I was in there for hours. There was no light and clothes of all kinds surrounded me, suffocating me. It was so dark. I remember I was screaming at the top of my lungs. One girl's mother came home, opened the door, and asked, "What's going on?" Those children laughed. I remember feeling very weak, and I was soaked with sweat and could hardly speak. I went home and told my mother what happened. She talked to the girl's mother.

My mom did the best she could, but she was locked in her own prison. We were hungry a lot. I would often visit the neighbor downstairs and ask for water. Once I looked in the sink and saw meat that was being thrown away. I grabbed it and ate it. Our lights were sometimes shut off for non-payment. We had no oil that heated the house, and so we were often cold. Mom would take me and my little sister to her friend's house so we could be warm, and she would give us food. I ate spinach straight out of the can, and it did not taste good. I went to other children's' birthday parties and wondered why I never had a party or a birthday cake. I didn't have any of my own birthday parties to remember.

After trying to tell my mother about the abuse, my stepfather got bolder and started doing other things. The abuse went on for eight or nine years. At night, I would make a tent around me with my dolls, put on two pairs of underpants and two pairs of pajamas, and I would tuck my sheets all around me, thinking he could not touch me. When I got older and he came into my room, I fought back. I would not pretend to be asleep. One night, I opened my eyes and said, "Stop!" He was drunk and ran from my room. He stopped coming near me, except when he was fighting my mother. Once I jumped to her defense. I yelled, "Leave my mother alone!" and jumped on his back. He pushed me off and slapped my face.

I ran from the house and pulled the fire alarm box. When I heard the sirens of the fire truck, I felt a powerful feeling. It put more fight in me. To this day, I have such respect for firefighters.

When I hear the sirens, something happens inside me. I get a sense of the power these men had when they came to help me. Firefighters in full gear with big helmets, large boots, oxygen tanks on their backs, and heavy looking raincoats had power, and they were there to save us from the sick drunk who I hated.

I became a fighter after that; he had nothing to say to me. I told him, "If you touch me or my mother, I am calling them again." I was about thirteen. He was still coming in drunk every weekend. I remember not wanting to leave my mother by herself.

My mother was a broken woman, afraid to be alone. She had stayed in boarding schools while my grandmother worked. She would say she felt no love growing up. So as a woman being abused, she held onto her kids, my older sister and me. She was always sick, keeping us home from school to be with her and telling us things we should not know. She would say my older sister was her comfort. She also kept me closer than she needed to. I became very sickly. I had nosebleeds, heart trouble, and asthma, and lived in a lot of fear. My brother was working all the time and gave her money for food.

I was never free from sick old men who loved babies. The man who I thought was my dad had a brother that would visit my mom and pick me up. I could feel his erection and told my mother. She believed me that time. She told him not to pick me up anymore.

When my mother had company, they had drinks and there would be beer in the refrigerator. I would open the cap and drink from the bottle until it was almost empty. I liked the taste. I was about ten years old.

I was sixteen when my mother said she wanted to tell me something. She said the man I thought was my father wasn't. She walked away from me and returned with pictures saying, "This man is your father." She gave me letters he had sent to her. I thought I would die and started crying. She said, "You were a love child. The man I had a love for was not who I thought he was, and it greatly disappointed me."

"What about my real father?" I asked.

She said he was married and had children. He had wanted to leave his wife, but she told him not to and that she did not want to break up his home. He was a handsome, mixed-race man, and she said I looked a lot like him with his beautiful smile. She also said to not feel sad. But I did. I felt like I did not belong.

I was attracted to gangsters like the ones I saw in the movies. I wanted to go away—just get away from her. I started ditching school when she would send me and wanted to find a job to make enough money to leave home.

One day, I left the house as if I was going to school and walked around the neighborhood looking for a place to work. There was a family-run sub shop near my home, and I wanted a job there. I asked the manager if he was hiring. He asked, "How old are you?" I told him I was sixteen. He told me I was too young to cook, but I could do the dishes, and I agreed.

My mother thought I was going to school, but I was working. I would do anything to be away from what was called home. It was a hellhole to me, and I hated being there. I quit school and told her what I was doing. Everything was falling apart. I became a sex object—young, fresh meat.

One day I was cleaning tables, and a man who came in everyday whispered in my ear and said, "I could bore a hole right through your panties." I ran into the kitchen and told my boss, pointing the man out. He told me to stay in the kitchen. My heartbeat so fast it felt like it was coming out of my chest. My boss went in the back to use the phone, and after hanging up, he walked to the front and stood behind the counter. I nervously watched from the back. It wasn't long before two men in black overcoats walked in. They looked at my boss, walked to the table where the man sat, stopped him from eating, and took him outside. The man's food stayed on the table. I peeked out to see if the man came back, but he never came back. Days went by, and I finally asked my boss what happened to the guy. He said that the man went on a vacation, and I didn't have to be afraid, he was never coming back again. He also told me to let him know if anybody else disrespected me.

DRUNK AGAIN

While walking home one day, I saw fire trucks parked on my street. From a distance, they looked like they were at my house. The lights flashed, and as I got closer, my heart raced. The firetrucks were at my house. I remember thinking, *Oh my God. Did he hurt my mother?* I was angry at her, but I wanted nothing to happen to her. As I walked closer to the building, the men brought out things that looked like charcoal in the shape of pillows and stuff that I recognized from my house. My stepfather had set the couch on fire, smoking.

I told my boss what happened. Again, it wasn't long when the same two guys that took care of my previous problem came to my house. They met me at the top of the stairs and asked what happened. I told them. Then they asked, "Where is he?" They found the culprit sitting on a chair with his feet up like all was well. Half the furniture had burned up, and the house smelled like smoke. The two men walked into the living room and told my stepfather to get it together, grow up, and to be a man. They also warned him that they did not want to come back to see him. After that, one man pulled his overcoat to the side, revealing his gun in a hip holster. The spokesman said, "If you ever touch the girl or your wife again, we will take you for a ride. Do you understand?" My stepfather was sweating. I had never seen such fear in a man before. He was soaked like he had just gotten out of the shower, and he was instantly sober. The visit straightened him out forever.

The image of the men dressed in black overcoats revealing his revolver burned a more lasting impression in my memory than the burned apartment. Those men telling my stepfather that they didn't want to take him for a ride changed everything in that house. My stepfather moved to New York. He would visit my mother once every two or three months. I was very happy to not smell alcohol and see his face.

THE ONE WHO GAVE
ME LOVE

The only part of my childhood that was safe and fun was when I was with my Nana. She was so beautiful, with long braids. She was born on an Indian reservation. I loved her so much. We would go shopping and have apple pie and ice cream. She bought me pretty ribbons for my hair, and I would spend the night at her house. I loved being with her. It was safe. I told her I was afraid of the dark when it was bedtime. She told me, "It's okay. I will put a little light on for you." When I was with my Nana, I did not feel the fear I felt when I was with my mother.

My grandmother was the only real loving person in my life. Once she got sick and needed a blood transfusion. I told some of the coffee drinking customers around the sub shop what had happened to her. One of them said, "I will get tested to see if I can give her blood." He immediately got up and said, "Let's go." We picked up my mom and went to the hospital. My mom and I waited for what felt like a long time to hear the results to see if he was a match. Finally, the man walked into the waiting room with a smile on his face. I held my breath, waiting for the answer. With an immovable smile, he said his blood was a match. We were at the hospital for hours. After giving his blood, he came out with that beautiful smile and said, "LaQue, you now have a full-blooded Italian in your family." At once, I felt protected and cared for. They were my family, not just because of his giving blood to my grandmother, but because they came to my rescue. Unfortunately, my grandmother later died. Some of the men came to the gravesite and then brought food to the house. They made sure that we were okay, like a family would. I didn't fully understand the impact they would have on my life.

A Troubled Teenager

After my grandmother's death, I had nothing to live for. One night, I cut both my wrists, thinking it was a way out. But in that process, I decided it would not solve anything. I went to the hospital where they referred me to a therapist. The therapist and I talked from time to time, and I felt better. Soon, I went back to work at the sub shop. They saw the marks on my wrists and asked, "What are you doing? You are a beautiful young lady with a lot to live for! What's wrong?" The family said, "Don't do that again!" They also told me to go back to school and to go out with boys my own age. My Italian family and the therapist helped me to focus and see myself differently. I read self-help books that told me to strive for what I want, and that I could do great things in life. I made a concerted effort to try.

MORE
DISAPPOINTMENTS

One day the sub shop was suddenly gone. The family had to close it. The building was empty and alone, and so was I. When I walked by the door and saw the big room with nothing in it, I would cry. There was no one to call or talk to when there was trouble. I lost my focus when dark and fearful memories and trauma would flood my mind. I was abandoned, with no one to turn to. Who could I call? I reflected on the few years that had passed, afraid of the dark. Darkness represented horror, and I had to sleep with lights on. I also had an involuntary choking reflex and a form of haphephobia. I didn't want anything to touch my neck. I didn't even like shirts or blouses that fit too tight. I remember thinking; *I want to grow up and become a woman, to leave home, and to escape the memories that made me so unhappy.* The life I knew as a child was horrible. I felt unloved.

I now had a whole new set of problems. I walked into the neighborhood bar looking for a job. I told them I was old enough to work there, but it lasted a very short time. They told me I could not work there, but instead I could hang out. When law enforcement came in, I was instructed to stay in the back. While there, I connected with a man who had no respect for me. He was only interested in my body. He was different from my Italian family, but he was in the same line of work. I was looking for love in all the wrong places and from the wrong people. I had hopes of finding what I once had in the men from the sub shop. Unlike this new crowd, they had wanted me to do well, had treated me with respect, and had provided protection.

Around this time, my mother and I moved into an apartment where there were all kinds of people from all walks of life. A lady came to us from the apartment across the hall and asked if I would babysit. She dressed in fur coats and drove big cars. She had a sister. I eventually put it all together. There were a few women like that in the building, so I started a babysitting business.

When I was 14, I was raped while babysitting by a person who was a friend of the family. My mother had told him to keep me company since the woman I was sitting for was a drunk, going out at night and bringing home strange men. This person was there to protect me, and my mother thought he was a good guy. He instead brought harm to me. I often thought of my mom who she put trust in. It was slanted. However, she would not believe me when I told her about her husband, who took advantage of me.

I got pregnant and started bleeding very badly. I just stayed in bed, and my mother said to stay off my feet and that would stop the bleeding. My mother brought me food and soup and checked my pad to see if anything came out. After about two months, the horrible pain and heavy bleeding stopped, and I stayed in bed about three more days. I started to feel better, but a week later, I took a bath and I felt more pain. This thing that looked like a yellow tadpole came out of me. I called for my mother, who came into the bathroom, looked at it, and said it was the baby.

The women that I babysat for treated me like a little sister, and one of them had a keen interest in me. Her name was Lorrie, and we spent long hours talking. She told me that she wanted to be a nurse, but she had to drop out of school and turned to prostitution to support her baby. She walked away from a bad relationship; she worked for herself, and she did not give her money to anyone. She helped me a lot as a young girl who needed to know how to care for myself and my body. I had not had that while growing up. The training she received in nursing school helped me with those questions a young lady has growing into a woman. She told me to go to school and get educated, and to not drop out like she did. She had a plan to retire so she could live a respectable life. After speaking with her, I told my mom I wanted to go to school to learn makeup and hair styling. She was indifferent. However, I was determined. I am grateful to that steadfast woman who took an interest in me. Because of her, I pursued my interests.

The training included a six-month course. However, with one month left in my training, the money ran out, and my mother told me I had to leave. I was crushed. I loved learning this art, and I was good at it. I met another woman that had dreams and took an interest in me as a troubled teenager looking to belong and find refuge. She wanted to give me the money to finish school. My mom said no; she did not want me to be beholden to the lady. She refused her offer to help me.

When I told Lorrie about my trouble and how discouraged I was, she told me to respect myself and not let men take advantage of me. She would say, "Love is not sex; it's more than that." I never forgot what she said to me. I was determined to take more classes and not give up because of her inspiring words.

NOT GIVING UP,
HEARING THE WORDS
YOU CAN

I was hungry for more and took more classes for hair and makeup. I worked in some shops located in the suburbs of the city that had training for wig and toupee styling. I was good at it, and many people said that I was a very talented artist.

I was also always in a nightclub. People of the night frequented the same places. For me, the streets were an escape. Those people all got to know me. If a drunk got out of line, one guy would say, "You watch your mouth. You respect her. She is a lady." The relationships reminded me of what I had before, the family that I no longer had or ever did see again. There was a new group that I saw all the time. I turned to alcohol to feel better. The lights, the music, the beautiful costumes, and the happy people felt like something I had never known before. There were sounds of laughter I had never heard until then.

Going out every night gave me something to look forward to. I didn't know I was going down a path that could lead to a point of no return. I was doing what the people in my Italian family had told me not to do. You may wonder how people of that lifestyle care for a troubled teenager? But they did. If they could have seen the path I was taking and who I was associated with, they would have said, "What are you doing? Go home."

But as fate would have it, another *family* came along and asked, "What are you doing out here? You're a nice girl. Why do you want to be out here?" If I had a little too much to drink, one of the guys would put me in a cab, pay the driver, and tell the cabbie to make sure I got home. He would eye the driver and say, "Wait until she gets in her door. Understand?" He would also take his taxi ID number. The drivers always did exactly that, certain that I got in my door.

I made the mistake of confusing small acts of kindness with love. It clouded my vision of trust. I got too comfortable. The night after the club closed, I was asked if I wanted to go to a party. All the dancers and some of the servers were going. When I was told the people I knew and thought I trusted were going, I felt it was okay. My brother's friend, who knew me when I was a kid, approached me at the bar. He said, "Look at you, all grown up!" He said he was going to the party too and not to worry. A person that I knew and *trusted* told me he would see me there.

While driving to our destination, this trusted man offered me a mint and said, "Don't chew it. Let it melt on your tongue." It was a long drive. I remember going over a bridge and that nothing looked familiar. We arrived at some kind of bar and walked in. I suddenly felt afraid. The people who said they were going to the party were not there. I asked where they were and didn't get much of an answer. I did see my brother's friend.

I sat at the bar and ordered a drink. I started to see things that were not there. I asked the guy who brought me there, "Did you see that?" He laughed and said no. I felt out of control. It was difficult to sit on the bar stool without swaying back and forth. I dropped a glass out of my hand. The man asked me if I wanted to lay down, telling me that there was a bed in the office, and it would be okay. He took me into the room and said I could lie down. My poor judgment and the betrayal of a family friend led to another dark place.

Taken Advantage Of Again

I was half passed out, and I could feel my clothes being taken off. I had lost all control and could hardly speak. I tried to say no, but I couldn't form the words. I remember seeing tall black figures all around me, and they did what they wanted with me. I don't know how long it lasted, but the sun eventually came up. The guy helped me get dressed, took me outside, put me in a cab, and he told the driver to take me wherever I wanted to go.

My mother was a praying woman. With all her faults and troubles, I believe God heard her prayers for me. She would sit in the window looking for me. I made it home that morning, feeling empty and worthless. I put her through the hell I was living in.

Things did not get better. I was still running around. Looking for what? I didn't know. I traveled out of the country to be with someone I did not know well. After leaving, I wanted to come right back home. Fear enveloped me.

I wanted to go to sleep and not wake up. But the words of the men from my Italian family resonated in my soul. They spoke words of encouragement. If they knew of my being used at this so-called party, it would have been bad for that guy. I was always looking to see if any of my family would appear to rescue me. Did they remember the blood that was given to my Nana? Did they remember the dirty pervert removed from the restaurant? Did they recall the stepfather who was told, "You bother her, we will go for a ride"? I remembered. I remembered them at the gravesite. I remembered their fancy black car, and the cars sent for our family to use from the funeral home. I remembered the food delivered to my house for people to eat after the service. They never took anything from me. They even told me to stop going out with one of the men that they knew, saying they were too old for me and that I should go out with someone my own age. I will be forever grateful to them.

As time went on, I thought about all they would tell me. I had to decide to live, not die. I had found the difference between sex and love. I learned to love myself, and I can love others with no effort.

When I look back, I don't remember asking, "Why is God allowing all of this to happen to me?" I came to understand that He does not inflict us with this way of life. There is evil in the world, and it shows itself in all kinds of ways, people, places, and things. Some ask, "If there is a God, why would he let this happen?" But my story will help you see how I met Jesus and why I have come to think the way I do. I knew He existed.

On my troubled journey, I was a young girl trying to find some form of deliverance, some protection, someone to save me. For what it is worth, the mafia family gave me a form of protection from what could have been more devastation or even the loss of my life.

OFF LIMITS

It was out. "Do not touch her."

Wherever I went in the nightclubs, there would be someone who knew me and knew who I knew. The pimps asked, "Who is her man?" They thought I was doing what the other women on the streets were doing. One of the pimps who had seen me with someone in the family said, "Don't you even look at her! She is a nice girl." When going out, I always sat at the horseshoe-shaped bar. I would sit in the middle of it where I could see the stage. I still could not stand to be home, but being out every night gave the wrong impression. On the other hand, sitting around the bar, drinking, and watching the entertainment made me happy. If anybody tried to pick me up, the bartender would say, she is not your type.

I became friendly with one of the dancers. She asked me what I did during the day. I told her I was looking for a job, and that I liked to do hair and makeup. She told me to come see her. She was a manager of a wig boutique, and they were looking for a stylist. I went to the shop, met with her, and after our interview, she gave me a couple of wigs to style. She was impressed and gave me the job.

I was so happy. We saw each other at the clubs where she danced at night. She was very nice; a lot of the people I met were nice to me. Some had professional jobs during the day, and worked as bartenders, waitresses, or dancers at night. I think I was the youngest one out there. I found out a lot about them, as everybody has a story to tell. I met different people from all over the state.

These new people asked me about myself while drinking and talking. They got to know a little more about me; I was transparent. They could see I was sincere. "You are one of us. Don't worry, no one will hurt you." At the end of the night, one man would walk me home. We talked about family vacations and the Italian culture, including the big family dinners. I had never had that kind of family gathering, and I wished I did. When I expressed this during one of our talks, the man responded, "I am Italian." He reminded me of my Italian family, the only people who felt like they were my family. I am very grateful to the men who did not take advantage of me. They would be very happy to know their words penetrated my soul and helped me to see who I could become. Their words taught me to not let what I went through define me.

Their words helped build me up.

"Go to school."

"Go home."

"You can do great things."

I was a lost young teenager who was looking for love in all the wrong places. I did not value my life, and I wanted to end it. But I was told I had a lot to live for.

Wherever you are, it's because of you. I am writing my story, and very grateful you took an interest in me. I am proud to call you my Italian family.

Meeting A Man Who Walked Into My Life Just In Time

DON'T POINT FINGERS - YOU DON'T KNOW THE STORY

I understand the young ladies who are living this life do it for many reasons. Some of those reasons could be part of my story. Some of those reasons include rape, incest, latchkey kid, alone with no love, or parents who are selfish and don't love themselves and could not love you.

Later, I was able to let everything go and not let those reasons hold me back from being everything I was told I could be. I continued to take classes and work while I was in school. When I was not working or studying, the only place I knew where I could be happy was the night clubs. The men I knew in my younger years were no longer around.

With all that I was exposed to, I was very unhealthy and not safe. I believe that my life had been a course of fate. There was divine intervention. I was on a path of destruction or maybe even death, not by my hand, but by being in the wrong place at the wrong time, with the wrong people.

One night, I went to an after-hours club, and while sitting at the bar, someone pulled out a gun and started shooting. We all dropped to the floor. I looked to find life, something far from what I had been experiencing. I wanted to know true love, but I was looking in the playgrounds of death and destruction. Thank God I walked away unharmed. After that shootout, I could not stop shaking. It took a lot of scotch to calm me down.

I just did not want to go home. I would do a double, stay up all night, go home, shower, then go to work. The next day, I would do it all over again. Not sleeping was the worst thing. I was so wound up that when I decided to stay in for the night; it was hard to fall asleep. My mind was always racing. I was overtired, and old thoughts would run through my mind. It was horrible, and I was always hung over from drinking too much.

While working at the wig boutique, I decided to dance at night for extra money to pay for makeup classes at the school. One day, while I was standing in the lobby of a hotel waiting to be called for an interview. A man approached me and said, "Hello. Are you here for the interview?" I answered yes. He introduced himself as Sonny, and I told him my name. He was good looking and had light-colored eyes. He asked if it was a French name. I said yes. He eyed my school uniform and asked me if I was a nurse. I told him no. He then asked, "Why do you want to dance in this place?"

I told him I needed money to pay for more classes. Just then, my name was called to meet the owner and show him my dance.

When I was done, Sonny waited for me in the lobby. He said, "Nice meeting you," and he gave me his business card, saying he was a club owner, and would like me to be his guest.

I never got a call back from the club where I interviewed. I waited until the weekend and took Sonny up on his invitation. He stood at the door when I arrived, and he escorted me to the bar. We had drinks, and he said we would get a table later when the show started. When he left, he told one of his friends to look after me. Later, he came back and escorted me to a table where his friends were sitting and introduced me to them. The show was amazing. At the end of the evening, he thanked me for coming out and asked if I would come again. I said yes. I gave Sonny my telephone number. He said he would call me. As the owner of the club, he had to close things down and could not take me home, but he gave a cab driver money and told him to take me to my address and wait until I got in my door. He took the cab driver's number.

A week went by, and he called to ask if I would again be his guest. He told me he would send a driver to bring me to the club. I agreed. When his big fancy car pulled up. All my neighbors in the projects had their heads out of windows, looking wide-eyed at the car.

When I got to the club, Sonny met me at the door and escorted me to a big table. The men sitting there stood up as he introduced me to each one. He pulled out my chair so I could sit. I had never had that kind of treatment, but the level of respect was reminiscent of my Italian family. I felt very special once again, and I was treated like a lady. It felt like a dream the way Sonny and his friends would treat me with such respect. He never tried to kiss me or touch me in any way.

We went out to dinner as an entire group of about fifteen people. I had a great time. Afterward, Sonny and his driver took me home. I thanked him for a wonderful evening.

He would call me from time to time and send a car to pick me up. I would go to the club, and when he had to walk away for whatever reason, he always had one of his friends stand behind me. He was never alone, and when I was at the club, neither was I.

Sometimes Sonny would call me to say he will be by to pick me up after work, be ready and we'd take a ride. He wouldn't tell me where we were going, and the ride would take a few hours. After a while, I would see a sign, "Welcome to New York." We would have breakfast and then go right back to where I lived.

I wondered if Sonny had something to do with me not getting the job. But it didn't matter because this was the beginning of an amazing life with Sonny Cinnoche.

I Believe God Put Up Another Roadblock To Save My Life

Sonny was interested in me from the first day he laid eyes on me. We talked about the art of makeup. He encouraged me to get my license, and he told me he would open a hair and makeup salon connected to a spa and boutique. He surprised me one night at the club with some business cards that he made for me with a hair design logo and my contact number. He sent me back to hair design school. He would pick me up and drop me off at class. I finished the program, and we celebrated by going out to dinner. He told the server to bring the best champagne to our table. I remember thinking, "Wow! Is this real?"

I felt so happy, an uncommon feeling. Happy had not been an emotion I previously experienced. He instructed all the ladies of the night to have me do their wigs. They would drop the wigs off at the club office. Friends of the women asked them who did their hair and wigs, and my card was passed around. Some of them wanted me to come to their homes, and they paid me extra. Sonny would not let me go alone. His driver would take me, and he waited for me to do the client's hair. If Sonny knew them, it was okay for his driver to drop me off and come back for me. I was always protected and never alone. Sonny would say, "Take care of Que." If I went to the ladies' room, someone was outside waiting to walk me back to where I was sitting. There was always a part of me who loved the attention. His group of associates had class. I never took a cab to the club. If he could not pick me up, he would call to tell me he was sending a driver.

One night, Sonny drove me home and asked me to be his girl. He told me if I said yes, there was a price. I could not go out with any other guys, and I had to cut all ties with the people I knew before him. I said yes! The next night around midnight he called and told me to get ready to be picked up because there was something he wanted me to see. When I got there, he had surprised me with designer clothes, suits, fur-trimmed coats, and dresses for me. From day one, Sonny was out to lavishly protect me.

He later admitted that he had told the man from the interview to not call me. He said he did not want me to dance at a gentleman's club.

Picking Up Where
The First Family
Left Off

Sonny's attention saved my life. When he took me home at night, he waited until I waved out of the window to show I was okay. One night after he dropped me off, I could not get into the hallway. It was blocked by yellow tape. The police said I could not go in, and in the hall, there was blood with white globs in it. I ran back to the car where Sonny was watching for me to wave out the window. I told him that someone had gotten shot. He said, "Let's get out of here!' He drove me to a hotel. "I won't take you back there tonight."

I called my mother to see if she was all right, and I told her I would be home in the morning. Later, the news reported that someone had been shot in the head. I lived in the projects where anything could happen, and it did. While Sonny and I had breakfast, we spoke about the business Sonny wanted to open for me. He suggested I take a business course. He asked me to look into it.

I got home around noon, and my mother told me the fire department came and washed up the remains. For days, you could smell blood. From then on, I was fearful about walking in the hall. So Sonny would walk me into the hall and see me into the apartment.

With this man in my life, I saw hope. I had a vision of what a good, clean life could be. What it would be like with a man who embraced me the first day he saw me, and who pulled me out of a hole. I told him how my life had been as a young girl. I told him about the teenager who was out of control, and the young woman who just wanted to be loved. He wanted to see the people who hurt me, like my stepfather, the friend of my brother who set me up, and the guy who used me. I didn't show him. I knew what would have happened. They would have disappeared like the guy in the sandwich shop. I don't know what happened to him, and I really did not want to find out.

I had peace of mind being with someone who loved me. Sonny would call and say, "I love you, Que." My heart would melt. I never heard anyone tell me that, not even my mother. We spoke every day. If I was not in class, I was with him. I did not want to be away from him. I felt safe.

A lot of the fear that I had lived with manifested at night. When we spent nights together, I would wake up yelling and jumping in my sleep. I would be drenched, like I had just taken a shower. One night, he reached for his gun, thinking someone was coming into the room. After learning what was going on, he held me tight and reminded me, "I will protect you. I am here." Then I would fall back to sleep.

This happened a lot. For years, I would put the bathroom light on in the hotel room when we spent nights together. After some time, he made me feel safe enough to shut the light off.

When I look back and see where I am now, I can see how God used Sonny to save my life. He held me close. There was no more going out with girlfriends to night clubs. However, one night a girlfriend of mine talked me into going out with her.

What a mistake that was. We sat at a bar talking, and a guy who I had seen before suddenly approached me from behind and tapped me on the shoulder. He said, "Sonny is outside and said come out to the car." I left my girlfriend sitting at the bar. I got into the car next to Sonny. He did not let me go back in. He was very angry, and he raised his voice and slapped my face, yelling, "You don't know who you were sitting with... you're gonna get us both killed." He had never hurt me or hit me before. I screamed and cried. I was in shock. When we got to his nightclub, he told me to stay in the car until he was done closing. I later found out the bartender called Sonny; he knew I was Sonny's lady. I did not know him, but he knew me. News travels fast.

Later that night, one of Sonny's friends who would pick me up and drive me to the nightclub had peeked into the window of the car while I was waiting for Sonny to come out. He asked, "Que, you okay?" I said nothing to him. I was heartbroken that Sonny had hit me. Sonny's friend waited with me in the car until Sonny came back. I believe he was told to come and stay with me. When Sonny returned, he held me and said he was sorry. He told me he would never hit me again. He kept his promise. After that night, he never did. I had no idea who I was sitting with to get him to that boiling point. I never went out for a girl's night out after that ordeal.

My girlfriend had called me the next day, wanting to know what happened. I told her that we were sitting with the wrong people is all. I told her to not ask me out again. I did not feel easy about going out, anyway. I was concerned that Sonny would not like it. As fate would have it, more was at stake than what I knew at the time.

When I read God's word, it says he will turn around what was meant for harm and destruction and use it for good. In the end, He will get the glory. At night, I would say my prayers.

Sonny would say, "Don't forget me." Whether I was sober or had a few drinks, I always fell to my knees by the bed. Sonny would wait for me to get into bed, and before falling to sleep, he would hold me tight and say, "Don't be afraid. I will protect you. I love you, Que." I would fall asleep in his arms. The night terrors became less frequent.

A little while later, I found out there was a barber and beautician fashion show with contestants from all over the state coming to town. Sonny wanted me to be a part of it. He told his barber friend to give me a spot. It was fantastic. I loved working with my personal model. I created a black and white affair; everything she had on was black and white, and I designed everything she was wearing. Half the hairdo was white and the other side black, and the model wore a jumpsuit with one black sleeve and one white sleeve. We did the same thing with the shoes; she was wearing one black and the other white. My design earned a standing ovation. At the end of the show, some of the guests congratulated me on such a unique presentation. I gave my business card to those who spoke to me. The show was amazing! Sonny waited for me when it was over. Afterward, we went to dinner and then to the club. It was a wonderful day and evening.

After a year or so, I was pregnant. I wanted a child, someone to love. Sonny was not happy, and he wanted me to get an abortion. He told me that he would take care of it. I said, "NO!"

One night, he sent his driver to pick me up. The driver told me Sonny wanted me to talk to someone. I went with him, but I was not comfortable. When we got to the destination, I would not get out of the car. The driver said, "Que, you just need to go in and talk to this man. Sonny told me to make sure I got you here." I didn't budge.

The driver called Sonny and told him I would not get out of

the car. Then he put me on the phone. Sonny told me the guy would give me a shot, and it would cause me to have my period.

I said, "No. I am keeping my baby."

"Put Ed back on the phone," Sonny said.

Ed drove me back to the club. Sonny came out to the car and said, "Que, this is not a good time."

I told him I didn't care, and that I had asked God for this child. I reiterated I needed this with or without him, no matter what. I told him he can do whatever he wants, even kill me, but I was keeping my baby.

We sat in the car for a long time, and he tried to convince me to give up the baby. Then he finally said, "Okay. This is it. Since you are going to have my baby, you must stop drinking, get rest, and take care of yourself."

At the time, I still lived with my mom in the projects. Every week he would bring me milk and juice, and go to the butcher for the best steaks, lamb, and other meats, including fresh vegetables. He said, "Our baby is going to be healthy." I did not want for anything because he provided everything that I could ever need and want.

I had a new mindset. I got all kinds of books about babies and childbirth, and no longer went out to the clubs. Sonny would come and take me out for rides after the club had closed for the night. I also went to child birthing classes.

Things started to change. Sonny pulled back from being with me for reasons he could not say. He would tell me, "Que, what you don't hear, you can't say. It's for your own protection that I don't see you for a while."

He had to leave the state, and I did not hear from him for a couple of months. A friend of his called me often to see how I was doing. He gave me no information on Sonny.

Finally, it was time to have my baby. I was admitted into the hospital. While in labor, a student nurse was assigned to me. I told her I felt like the baby was coming and her response was, "You are doing good, keep breathing." I grunted and pushed the baby out. The student nurse lifted the sheet and ran out, screaming, "Doctor, doctor!" The doctors and nurses came running in. When they lifted the sheet, my baby was crowning.

With a few big pushes, the baby came fast, right in the bed. They took my baby out of the bed and put it in a hospital crib. Then they rolled us both to the operating room, stating that I needed to be repaired and given something for the pain. I wasn't sure what had happened. I asked, "What is it?" Someone said you have a beautiful baby girl. While waiting for the epidural to work, one nurse said, "Look at your baby girl." and she rolled her closer to me. I saw the most beautiful little girl. She was so peaceful, just lying there looking around. She had light skin, big brown eyes, and a full head of brown hair. I looked at her, and our eyes met. She looked at me as if to say, "Hi, Mom." Just moments old, and she had her hands in front of her face, looking at them together as if folded in prayer.

After I was given the spinal, I was instructed to lie flat for a few hours, but someone lifted me up too soon, making my head hurt for days. What a night! They took care of me. I went to a room to recover, and they took the baby to the nursery.

Sonny had walked into my life, made my prayer come true, and fathered a beautiful little girl who changed my life. It was as if winter had gone, and summer had come; birds were singing and all the pain that had been in my life had melted away.

Soon after, I came home from the hospital, Sonny called and said he had heard I had the baby and asked how we were doing. I told him she looked a lot like him. He said he would have someone call to see if I needed anything. This little girl gave me so much hope, love, and comfort. I made a choice to be the best mother a woman could ever be.

I was grateful to Sonny for protecting me from myself, from the things I was exposed to, and from his lifestyle. If there were any conversations that he did not want me to hear, he would send me to the ladies' room. From day one, he had a concern for me to see that I lived free from harm and encouraged me to pursue a career. I see the hand of God in meeting this man. It's amazing how God used unusual angels to save a life and bring my story to life.

Sonny and I talked many months after our daughter's birth. He had to stay away and did not want to come near us. Three years had passed, and I got a call from him. Our daughter was turning four, and he wanted to see us. He came to my home to see his daughter. He said she was beautiful, and we talked for a while. He was sorry, but had to stay away. I agreed it would be best for him to continue to stay away. This little girl gave me a life I never thought I could have, and I wanted to give her the best possible future. I was ready to walk away from all potential harm. I never talked to him again.

Wherever you are, Sonny, thank you. Not only for saving my life through our relationship, but for fathering a beautiful daughter who was an angel for me. Being a mother is like breathing. It's wonderful. Thank you!

DISCONNECTION FROM
ALL THAT I KNEW - NO
MOB GUYS FOR
PROTECTION

With a renewed mind, I moved to a new project. I took a step in the right direction, starting with my living situation. I enjoyed motherhood and making a suitable environment for my daughter. I still lived with my mom and little sister, but I found a job that was in a wealthy area with people who had money to spend.

I worked in a fur and wig boutique with a specialty service. I worked toward a good life for me and my daughter, not asking anyone for a dime. I valued myself, asking God to help me be the best I could be. I continued to work and take classes to advance my makeup and hair styling skills. I customized the hair piece or wig to fit men and women who had sickness or natural baldness and wanted to improve their appearance.

One of my clients asked me to go on a European vacation, another to Paris. There were great opportunities I had to turn down because I was caring for my daughter. I was working to create a healthy environment. She was my number one priority. I searched for anything I could to better myself. Along the way, I made some mistakes. I was still learning the character of people, some good and some not so good. I associated with many people who were in business for themselves, and I was shadowing them, hoping to become that salon owner Sonny wanted me to be.

I met many men, married and single, that showed interest in me. I wondered if I had "sex object" written across my forehead. I learned a lot about business and about my self-worth. I was reminded of who I can be and what I can do. I remembered the women who said I could do great things with my life. I held on to the value and the lessons taught to me while sitting at a bar.

I never wanted my daughter to experience what happened to me. I wanted to protect her as best I could. I wanted to give her everything I had not received.

Just because you never had something in life does not mean you cannot learn to give what you never had. That is just what happened with God's help. I prayed and thought about all I never experienced as a child, teenager, and woman. I was around wholesome people who worked hard and made a life for themselves. The people I was with had families, and I learned some positive things. I used what I could and threw out the rest. I gained some valuable information from people from all walks of life. I learned to want a better life, and I could see the path others had chosen for themselves, but sometimes, it became a dead end.

MOVING - FINDING A NEW PLACE, OUT OF THE PROJECTS

I found an apartment in an area that was populated by Jewish and Afro-American residents. I saw a lot of shops in the area that specialized in African American styles such as dashikis and jewelry, styles that sparked my interest in trying something new. I applied for a business loan to open a boutique. My life has been about chances, so why not take a positive one. I went to a bank in the area that was giving out loans to people in the community who wanted to open businesses.

One thing I held onto from my old life is boldness and fearlessness. The boldness of my Mafia family attracted me to them. It represented power to me: the body posture, black overcoats, suits, black sunglasses, and luxurious cars. Through the eyes of a teenage girl who had nothing and no one to guide, love, or protect her, their image was powerful looking. This was the kind of man who protected me, and it made me feel powerful as well.

When I went to the bank, they gave me $40,000 to start, wanting to see how I would do. I researched where the New York City garment and jewelry district was, and I took a bus there, having never been before. With a New York City Yellow Pages, I stayed all day, setting up contacts. I started a boutique with African imports and American jewelry, a makeup line, wigs, and hair braiding, and put on fashion shows. I did very well.

The only time I went to the clubs was for my fashion shows to present my boutique items. I had my own personal models working with me, and I visited New York City to buy goods. The banker was surprised at how well things were going. Some people had told me the money I had was just enough to fail, but business was good. It was a small shop, but it worked.

I met other business owners in the community. One owner had a men's boutique and was the director and owner of a modeling school. He offered me a scholarship to train if I would give him a year's commitment to work for him as a model instructor. After being trained to teach students, I was required to attend extensive training for the instructors to teach the course to others. He made me head instructor. I received a diploma from the state board and a teaching certification.

Having my boutique and being in the public eye, I met a lot of people. Some of them were full of themselves and cared nothing about others. I learned who the takers were.

One taker was a man who taught self-defense, and I was interested in learning the art. We became friends only to find out he was interested in my prosperity as a young woman. This guy was a professional student who never graduated. I went with him and a girlfriend who was dating his friend on a weekend trip to his home state. My girlfriend had two girls, and I took my daughter. They took us to their dorm apartments. He dropped me and my daughter off and said he would be back shortly. But he didn't show up for two days. There was no food, and I was in a strange place with no transportation and no windows in the room. The basement had vending machines, so that was our food for two days.

I didn't have street smarts then, and I was disappointed in myself. How could I be a part of this craziness? I did not know where my girlfriend was. We did not talk. This person called the room next door to where I was staying. I told him to come right away and take me and my daughter to the bus station. I could not believe how stupid I was to expose my little girl to this. The taker asked me not to go, explaining he had business to take care of and could not get away. I won't say what word I used. I was a different kind of bait. All this kind of guy wanted was sex, and he could only see dollar signs with me. I never talked to him again. I have made mistakes, and that was one of them.

I still took self-defense classes and learned how to throw a man over my shoulder. It made me feel pretty good. There was a lot of violence in the city, so it was a good thing for me to know. After getting rid of all the dead weight, I continued to seek education. I went to night school to take business classes. I wanted to learn as much as I could. I also went to another university and received certification to be a consultant.

I learned the art of makeup application and went to New York City to connect with a fashion model who designed her own makeup line. The presentation was positive, and I featured the line in my boutique. I was qualified to teach makeup application and modeling. I combined everything I learned and was teaching the teachers hairstyle and wardrobe consulting. I put on fashion shows around the city.

Business was doing well until I decided to expand. Big mistake. The bank gave me more money. I had done well with what they gave me the first time, so I went to them with a proposal for expansion. The banker was impressed, so we went forward. It was not enough, but I took it anyway.

I needed another salesperson and bookkeeper. But I could not give myself a paycheck. I lasted one year in this new location and had to get out. I was around businesses that could charge less than I could, making it difficult to survive. I was sad to close my doors. My living conditions were where I wanted them to be, and I was raising my daughter in a very nice neighborhood. I did not look at this as a failure. I had stepped out and took chances. By doing so, I opened doors to new and better opportunities. I proved to myself that there is nothing too hard. All you must do is step out. If you fall, get up and try again. I was happy about what I had accomplished.

Turning Over A New Leaf

After the business folded, I did some modeling myself. I connected with a company and went to different stores to demonstrate the product. I was promoting a certain beverage, and at one location, I met the salesman who was a representative for his distributor. We spent the day advertising, and at the end of my shift, he told me he would keep me in mind for future advertising. He would ask for me at the agency.

A few weeks went by, and I had not received my paycheck. I called the location where the promotion was held and requested the number for the sales associates. The word got back to that salesman that the company had not paid me, so he called me and said he would look into it. He said a check had gone out to the agency that sent me to the job. I finally got paid, and the salesman asked me if he could see me outside of work. We talked a lot on the phone, getting to know each other. Then, we started dating. He would invite me to a lot of company events.

We saw each other regularly, and after two years, he asked me to marry him. I asked my daughter, who was eight at the time, what she thought. I asked if she wanted him to be a part of our family. She said yes; I told her she did not have to call him Dad.

We married, and it was not long after that I had another child, a son. My daughter loved her baby brother and was like a little mother to him. As time went by, she ended up calling my husband, Dad. She loved him. He was respectful, and I trusted him to be around her. With my background, trust does not come easy.

We outgrew our apartment and moved into a townhouse with much more room. Three years later, I had another son. And three years after that, I had a third son. We outgrew the townhouse.

I was a housewife and proud mother of four children. I loved every moment of it. I wanted it all and made it a point to read as much as possible. I went to women's groups who had families and children, and I had a lot of support. I even made my own baby food.

My husband told me to look for a home big enough for our family. We moved into a beautiful, large ranch house out of the city. We had an in-ground pool and plenty of room for the children to play, including their own basketball hoop. I planted flowers and vegetables. I loved my new life. Our home was in a cul-de-sac, so we did not have to worry about fast cars zipping by.

We met great people and their children. The moms stayed home when the men worked, and we had lunch together. I learned how they lived, and it taught me the same principles. They would come to our house, or we would go to theirs. Our children played sports together, and they had play dates. We would have dinners, pool parties, cookouts, and other get-togethers. When my children got out of school, I was home waiting for them with cookies in the oven. I played with them, took them to swimming lessons, and to the park. We watched television together, and they would tell me about school.

We sat down every night for dinner as a family. On Sundays, my children helped set the dinner table. It would be like a holiday. I made it to be special. I had never lived like this before, with water goblets, dessert forks, cloth napkins, fabric tablecloths, and candles in the centerpiece. I taught my daughter how to cook and taught my children to never go down the path I went down. I taught them to never make the same mistakes I made.

I told them the truth about a lot of my life, so they knew what not to do and what to be aware of. I told them to keep that information to themselves. They had sex education from me, not from school, or from some outsider who came to the school. I would not send them when there was sex education. I gave them what they needed at that time, at whatever age they were, so they did not have to learn from strangers like I did.

My New Focus

My daughter grew to be a wonderful young lady. Learning came easy to her, and she took swimming and tennis lessons at fourteen. She helped her brothers with school projects. They were all excellent students. My boys loved sports. My children mean the world to me and have been a great blessing.

I was very protective of my boys and my daughter. When she was fourteen, she was friends with a young man who wanted to date her. I told him he had to wait until she was older. He later became a part of our family. He would come to visit us to get out of the city and was a part of family night that included watching movies, playing games, and having pizza and popcorn. On the weekend, after the boys' games on Saturday morning, there was time set aside for everyone to be a part of cleaning the house, cutting the grass, trimming the shrubs, and cleaning the pool. After a hard day, we would fire up the grill, and everyone had a great time in the pool.

I called my daughter's friend my other son. We all fell in love with him. He spent a lot of time with us. My daughter was a part of saving my life and giving it meaning, and when the second child came, it was a blessing to have a man child; what a special gift. Then number three was spectacular, and number four was amazing. Every boy had very special gifts that added to my life to complete wholeness; each one had unique personalities.

They all displayed a love for me, that was very fulfilling, and made me parent with a purpose, to give them stability, self-worth, confidence, encouragement, and to learn what character means. I taught them to know the importance of giving your word. It has to mean something and develops who you are.

I used to tell them, if they did something wrong, just tell me the truth at all costs, no matter what. I did not tolerate lying. Night life was a thing of the past, and when I think of how it was for me growing up, I did not want that for my enemy.

My daughter could not babysit or spend the night in anyone's home except her grandmother's. Mothers must be careful who their little girls babysit for. At the time, my mom had no unhealthy people around. The boys did not spend the night anywhere. Most of the time, I encouraged their friends to come to our home. There were only one or two people that they could spend the night whom we knew very well.

In raising my children, I made a note of everything positive, so I could teach it to my children. Now I used the buddy system, so wherever they went, two of them had to go together. If they went to the movies and needed to use the bathroom two went together. I would drop them off and pick them up. I told them to sit only by families and other children. I wanted them to use what they had been taught. When they came home from school, I was there waiting for them. When their father came home, dinner was ready. Parenting with purpose was my goal. I gave them what I never had.

Think about what you would have wanted as a kid, and that is your teacher.

Don't do the wrong that was done to you.

My kids were signed up for sports every season—tennis, basketball, soccer, football, and Boy Scouts. Their father went on camping trips with them. They all had swimming lessons starting at two years old until they could swim in 10 feet of water. We went faithfully to the YMCA to take lessons and to the beach. There was no way for me, or anyone, to pass on fear to them. I made certain my children lived a wholesome, fearless, happy life, with character, courage, honesty, respect, and kindness to one another. We taught the boys to respect women, open the door, help with bags, and if they saw a woman who needed help, they knew what to do.

We all looked forward to winter and summer vacation. We rented a cottage up north for winter sports. On school vacations, we rented a camper to take road trips to Florida. Sometimes we went as a family to the Caribbean and to hotels for fine dining.

My husband was on the same page about teaching them the right way and exposing them to families who lived the way we did. Their father was a great provider. He worked all the time, so when the kids had a problem, they came to me. I told them the truth, and they knew it. I taught them manners: thank you, no thank you, please, and may I. They had to ask if it was okay to go over to someone's house and we had to know the parents, what they did for a living, and what standards they lived by. Most of the time, we were the host home for pool parties and sleepovers. I felt more comfortable with them sleeping in their own bed. When you have lived a life of horror, you make sure that you cross all the T's and dot all the I's, check and double-check everything inside and out, question who was going with them, what time the event was over, and which parent was picking them up. I knew the kids who were friends with my children, and I got to know their parents. We had dinner parties with them and visited each other's home with the children, cookouts, and pizza gatherings after a game. We all had a glorious life.

Seeing my children grow into teenagers and young adults, I thought about my life as a teenager, and young women, I was a train wreck waiting to happen. Until that day, a stranger walked up to me, introduced himself, he changed my life forever. I can look back and say, Thank You God!

MY DAUGHTER'S EXAMPLE

God has blessed me to be the mother of these wonderful human beings. My daughter loved me very much. When I got sick, she would get her comforter and lay down on the floor beside me, watching television, making herself available to me. She was like a second mother to my boys, as young as she was.

When my first son was born, a next-door neighbor invited me to church. I went, and that's when my whole life changed beyond my imagination. It is when it all came together for me. I learned about Jesus Christ. I would go every Sunday to learn the word of God. I was a sponge, wanting to learn as much as I could. I pieced my life together and found purpose. My daughter went to Sunday school, and my children learned about Jesus and God.

I did not blame God for all the bad things that happened to me. While going to church, I found out that there is evil in the world and some people follow that practice. There are people in the church who don't have the heart of God, and some of them act evil as well. So, I left. I did not go to church for about a year.

The mother of my daughter's friend, who I now call my son,

invited my daughter to her church, and the two of them would go together. One Sunday after church, my daughter said she, her friend, and his mom were going to be baptized. She asked the whole family to come. I liked the church a lot. My boys and husband enjoyed the service as well. We all went as a family every Sunday. The people were kind and loving, and the pastor was amazing. One Sunday, there was an altar call for those who would like to be a partner, join the church, and to have prayer. We all walked up to the front as a family. It was a beautiful service to see my daughter and her friend baptized together. After church, we would come home and have a family Sunday dinner.

As time went on, my daughter joined the choir. She looked beautiful in the red with white trim robe that they wore. I was on time to see her walk down the aisle, as 30 to 40 people took their place to sing. It was so beautiful!

I changed churches, but my daughter remained at the church we all once attended. I wanted more of God's word. There was a radio minister I listened to, and one day my husband said, "The man you listen to on the radio is visiting a church nearby. Do you want to go see him?" We did, and I liked him a lot. We started visiting his church, met his wife, and liked the teaching. The ministry had a lot of programs, including Bible teaching, and I attended the Bible School for two years. My daughter would visit my church from time to time, but she liked where she was.

God became central to my life.

Loss Is A Part Of Life

My husband was another blessing who walked into my life, fathered my daughter, and gave me three great sons. We were married for over 20 years, and he was a good father to all our children and a good husband.

Life as I had known it ended. My health was declining because my body was responding to the panic that I lived with most of my life. I started getting migraines. I could see our marriage was coming to an end. We grew apart. I had stomach problems and body pain. My new world had crumbled, and confusion set in. I could not think straight. Despair turned into anger. I could feel myself getting stronger mentality. The fight of survival returned. The survival mode I had before kicked in, like when I jumped on the back of that sick person who stole my purity as a child. I ran out and pulled the fire alarm. That kind of fight returned to my being, and my boldness was returning. I wanted to be married forever, but divorce proceedings took place.

I took a part-time job on the weekends and some night shifts. My daughter said little, but she knew a lot was wrong. The close family dynamics were gone. I remember a card my daughter gave me. It said:

"Place your trust in God's great care. When troubles come your way, take comfort in His presence, for he is with you every day. When you feel you need encouragement or need someone to guide you, just turn to God. He meets each need. He's always there beside you. This is just a note to let you know you're being thought about. *Love you.*"

She also gave me a beautiful array of flowers. She would often do that, as she was a very thoughtful girl who loved me as much as I loved her. She did not know that she helped to save my life.

When my daughter was 26 years old, a week before Christmas, I mentioned we had not had any mother and daughter time. She and I were both busy. I felt our time was fleeting. She said, "Mom. We can have a late breakfast today before I go to work." So we went to a place that we had gone to as a family. We had a great meal, shared each other's food, and laughed. We talked about her brother's basketball game the night before, which had a tribute to a teammate who had died. The team gave the mother flowers and offered a moment of silence before the game. We talked about how sad it was. I said to her it must have been hard for that mother who lost her son, and that I'd never known that kind of loss, losing a child.

We finished our food and talked about what Christmas decorations she was going to pick up for me from the store, and how she and her friend would get the tree. She said, "Don't worry, Mom. You have to work late. I'll get the things." That night she was going to a Christmas party with a friend. She did not drink, so she was the driver. The boy who loved her so much had asked her to marry him, and the wedding was scheduled for the following March.

We kissed goodbye, and she ran out of the restaurant ahead of me, as she had to hurry. I waited to get my change from the waitress. When I went out the door, I was expecting to see her driving off, but there was no sign of her leaving the parking lot. I was left with an empty feeling, like she had never been there with me.

About two o'clock that morning, the doorbell rang. It was a police officer. I buzzed him in. He asked, "Do you have a daughter?" I answered yes and my heart stopped beating. I asked why, and he said she was in a car accident and was killed. He needed me to go to the hospital to identify her. He said he was sorry for my loss. I asked what happened, and he said she hit the tree head on. *After a beautiful day of us being together, how could this be?* The officer asked if there was someone who could take me to the hospital. I said I would find someone. I remember asking if her face was messed up. He said as far as he knew, no.

First responders at the site of the accident had tried to revive her. They had to use the jaws of life to get her out of the car. The girl who was with her was taken by air flight to a Boston hospital and expected to live. I asked the officer, "Are you sure it was my daughter, and not the other girl?"

He said, "Yes, sorry. It is your daughter. We have her identification, and you are the contact person in the event of an emergency."

Later, I found out she had fallen asleep at the wheel, driving 30 miles an hour and drove into a tree. She was taking her friend home after the Christmas party. I was blessed to have her in my life for 26 years.

After the police officer left, "I called my pastor's home and told his wife what had happened. She asked me if I needed someone to go with me. I said yes, and she sent the associate pastor who came right away.

It was close to four in the morning when we went to the

hospital to view her body with her boyfriend and two of her brothers. When I walked up to the table she was on, I could hear the machine that kept her warm. I asked if she suffered. The medical staff said no, it was quick.

I was learning about the ministry of Jesus Christ and him praying for people that recovered, so I started praying. The pastor touched my shoulder and looked into my eyes. He shook his head as if to say no. I lifted the sheets because I wanted to see all my sweet daughter, her hands had blood on them. Her nose was cold. I kissed her. She looked like her beautiful self, with no marks on her face. She had a peaceful look. I imagined God's angels escorting her into heaven. I kissed her goodbye and told her I loved her. I also told God I did not blame him.

We left the hospital, and the pastor stayed with me the whole day until after supper. My pastor's wife came as the associate pastor left. She did not say much, but she sat with me and held my hand. Sometimes words are not necessary. Having a body there helped and provided comfort.

It was one week before Christmas, and the day before one of my son's birthdays. He did not want a cake, and they did not want to celebrate Christmas. Their sister was the one who loved Christmas. She would wear Christmas tree earrings, a Santa hat, and a sweater that had a reindeer on it. I had to take the bull by the horns and say, "We are going to celebrate Christmas. We will buy a tree and decorate it, and we will have cake and ice cream for your brother's birthday." We did just that. I had to lay down my grief and keep the boys focused on how we had to keep it together. We even went to a Christmas event at the church. The young man she was going to marry was with us.

After the shopping and decorating. I had to concentrate on planning the funeral and sending my daughter home to be with

Jesus in heaven. I went to see my old pastor, her current pastor, and I explained why I had left his church. He respected my choice and accepted our wish to have the service at his church. I asked him to let me speak to the choir director and have them sing what my daughter liked to sing with them. I made certain they were happy uplifting songs–no depressing songs. He let me play secular music in the background and Christmas carols by female artists, like a popular concert. Then I had to buy what she would wear. Since it was Christmas, I told the florist to place red and white poinsettias all around her white casket. I put presents inside it with some reindeer. I did not want it to look dull. I had bunches of balloons at both ends of her casket. It was amazingly beautiful.

So many people came. There was no room in the sanctuary. People stood out in the entrance way. The school had a bus for each sports team the boys played on–football, basketball, and soccer. The football team carried the casket. The students from Bible school came, along with the teachers and associate pastors and some members of the church as well. It was wonderful. The whole idea was to celebrate her life.

This was the hardest thing I ever had to face, the love of my life killed, removed from the face of the earth. I thought what I had gone through in my early life was hard! My heart was in little pieces, and it was hard to breathe. My chest felt like a heavy weight was on it, and I felt numb, with no feeling in my body. I wondered if I could survive. Would this kill me? The boys needed me, and we needed to go on. I loved them enough to let go and focus on them. My daughter was gone, and they were still here. I loved them very much! There was so much more to lose. I could not be selfish, not knowing if I wanted to live. This girl and her dad were responsible for my life being renewed, and they had saved me from the clutches of vultures, looking for young girls. Sonny turned my life around and fathered a beautiful little girl who had brought new breath into my lungs. Oh, the joy of knowing her! The boys loved her so very much, and she was dedicated to her brothers.

LIFE HAS OBSTACLES TO OVERCOME

Before my daughter died, she went with me to see a house. She said, "Mom, there is not enough room for all of us. There is just enough room for you, Dad, and the boys." I told her we could take the basement and make it into another room and a sitting room. I remember the look of disappointment on her face. After her death, I felt bad. I can still see the look on her face and hear her words. We were trying to hurry the process of buying this house.

After her death, I had to break down her bedroom. The police station and the hospital returned the clothes she was wearing at the time of the accident, which still had blood on them.

No one was around to help me pack up the house and get things ready for the move. I also picked up the boys from school. I would lie in her bed as often as I needed to and feel comfort. At the same time, I did not want to disconnect from my boys who needed me. I had to pull it together, pack up her bedding, and put everything in bags to move. It's amazing what money does. It changes things and destroys relationships. We had to come up with a higher down payment. And money for renovating the basement to create another bedroom. It was only a two-bedroom house, and the carpenter finished off a room that could be another bedroom, which had previously been a dirty basement.

The carpenter was a soccer dad and friend of the family. Our boys played together. He helped us out as much as he could, but it was still a big expense. The money was running out. We passed papers and had to give them the amount they wanted for the down payment, which was more than what I was told in the beginning. The closing costs made the money thin. We could not move in right away, as the carpenter said it was best for him to finish his work first. However, time was running out, and we had to get out of the apartment. I thought a week or more in a hotel would be the cost of us taking a short trip, and I asked everyone what they thought. All were in favor of booking a trip to a warmer climate.

After a week's time, the carpenter had everything finished. We returned home, got everything out of storage, and moved in, including all that beautiful furniture from our other home and my daughter's wedding shower gifts. We tried to get back to what we knew was normal, but it was not happening. There was still such a big hole in our lives.

One night after everyone went to bed, I watched the late news that featured rescues by first responders. I could not believe my eyes. They were talking about accidents that required the jaws of life to rescue people. I watched the fire department remove my daughter from the vehicle she had been in. I shook, and my heart exploded out of my chest. Everyone was in bed, and I was all alone. I called the television newsroom and told them they did not have my permission to keep showing that. That it was my daughter I had lost. At first, it was shown during the daytime news, but they continued to show it, and that was not good. I did not want my sons to see that. The news supervisor said he was sorry, and they would remove it from the stream of events

We lived there for about two years. As things were declining, the monthly storage payment was falling behind. I was at the end of the program in Bible school. The graduation was great, and I got a diploma for the two-year program.

We got through that difficult time. To keep my daughter alive in our hearts, we celebrated her life every year on her birthday with dinner and cake. I would get flowers and balloons for the table. At the end of the evening, we would go outside, release the balloons, and watch them float far, far away while singing "Happy Birthday." Stars would be out, and it was a very special time.

Life is not the same without her. We are affected in different ways.

For me, it's like walking. My foot was broken and has healed, and I can do a lot of things, but it's not the same as before. Sometimes it hurts when it rains, but it does not stop me from doing what I must do. The scar reminds me of the repair that I needed. God's grace keeps me going and has not left me without the love of a daughter. As God would have it, young ladies have walked into my life who look to me as a mentor and mother. One day, the spiritual sisters will meet this beautiful girl who filled my life with so much love, which I can share with the many daughters from different mothers. I have compassion for young girls and teens who have gone down the same path that I once walked. When I think of everything that happened to me, it's a wonder I could still stand. But God continued to hold me up. I read the Bible to look for encouragement and the support from my church held me together.

While trying to keep things together, the man I once thought to be my father died. One year later, my mother died. I had to stop and regroup from the funeral of my mother. It felt like everything was falling apart. I could not continue to pay the mortgage. The time had come, and we all needed to leave the house. This bothered me because it was my daughter's life insurance policy that got us into this house, and we had to leave. I needed to put the rest of our things in storage, and I found a real estate agent.

We held an open house. Every day, strangers were walking through the house. I felt my privacy was invaded when I came home. The house finally sold. So, with what was left from the house, I needed to find an apartment. The buyers wanted to move in right away and did not give me the time I needed to find a place. They had a deadline. The only thing to do with the boys was to move into a hotel while I found an apartment and put everything in storage. That was more money that had to be paid out. Now I had two storage rooms, one that held most of my things from the larger house, and the other held the furnishings from the house we were moving from. We stayed in a hotel for a short time, while the landlord put a rush on cleaning up our new apartment in another town.

While going through divorce proceedings, agreements were put in place for the future. However, it did not work out the way it was supposed to. It made me look like the bad person, and I was accused of wrongdoing. In the eyes of my sons, I tried to keep what was going on to a limit and did not want them to carry my burdens. They were going through enough. Trying to protect them, and not to lose my focus, I had to do the best I could for all of us.

Divorce is like a death. It not only affected me, but my son's as well. With the loss of my daughter and their sister, it was very hard. I tried to help them keep it together and provide stability. I tried to focus on the fight I was in for my own health and well-being, including emotions running high of sadness, anger, and the feelings of disappointment from a failed marriage.

Once we moved into our new place, I tried to make it as much like home as possible. I had to buy bunk beds for the boys. It was a two-bedroom apartment, much smaller than what we were used to. Meanwhile, I was concerned where the boys would go to school and that it be the right decision. My pastors worked out a plan for me, so they could attend the school that was a part of the church. Leaving their friends was not easy, and this separation was very hard on them. The school worked out a monthly plan for us. With all the monthly payments that I was confronted with, there was hardly anything left.

We lived there for about three years. I found a job to help with everything and sold some of the things in storage, like the washer and dryer, to pay the storage bill. The storage company told me if I did not pay the full amount, they would sell my things, and they did. They sold the beautiful furnishings from my first home. Everything in storage meant a lot to all of us, including the boys' trophies, my daughter's shower gifts, and things that could not be replaced. Everything had to be sold, gone forever. So much loss, but God made my heart strong. I was able to get through it.

I remember the story of Job in the Bible, who lost everything, even his children, to death. His health was under attack, but he was faithful to God. His friends mocked him, his wife was not supportive, and she yelled, "Why don't you curse God, and just lay down and die?" But Job had faith in God. He did not fall under the pressure from all that was around him. Job, chapter 42, verse 10. The lord turned the captivity of Job. At the end of all that he went through, God gave him twice as much as he had before. His children had died, yes, they were gone, but he had more children; everything he had was multiplied. Job believed:

GOD WAS AND IS: PROVIDER, HEALER, BURDEN BEARER, COMFORTER, PEACE GIVER IN THE STORM!

In reading the Bible story of this faithful man of God, it helped me to hold on to faith and that God would not forsake me, even when it seemed impossible to get through. I felt I was losing so much that was dear to me. It was my faith in the All-Mighty God that held me together.

He brought me through what seemed to be the valley of death before, and he will do it again.

I thought some would be with me, through thick and thin, but they were nowhere to be found.

Out of the blue, I got a notice from the landlord saying he was going to raise the rent. The increase was so drastic that there was no way I could pay for it. The time came that we had to leave the apartment. The boys and I had to separate. They went with people who turned out to be friends in this time of need, and I moved into a rooming house for women in transition. It was a very small room, but I was grateful. I had some of my things in the trunk of my car because the room could not hold everything. There was no closet space. There were several women on each floor, with one bathroom and a shower. I still had my job as a consultant, and having the job helped me keep it together.

We lived like this for one year. I continued to look for afford-able housing while working, and the boys kept it together while staying with friends. One day, I got a call from someone asking,

"LaQue, are you still looking for an apartment?" I said yes, and my heart beat with excitement.

She said, "I have an apartment for you. Can you come in and fill out the paperwork?" My God! I couldn't believe it, but it was true. I met this lady the next day, gave her the down payment, and made move-in plans. I told the boys, and they were happy that we would be together again. Only two of the three boys came with me. A family once again, but not like before. Things had changed forever. I am grateful the boys were older and could understand. They would have loved for all of us to stay together, but they accepted the fact that things had changed. I learned that in life, we must make decisions that we may not want to make. In the end, it works out, and we have to live with it. Our lives changed drastically and forever.

Once we were settled in the apartment, one of my sons married. After a few years, the second son moved to another state, while the other one remained with me. It's not the ranch home with the in-ground pool, but it's comfortable, and I have peace.

The divorce from my husband was finalized. We see each other around the holidays to be with the boys. We were married for over 20 years and raised a great family.

I continued to work, doing what I love to do. Teaching and life skills coaching, as well as motivational speaking. I worked at a modeling school as an instructor, and I traveled statewide, attending youth programs, schools, and colleges. I remained at the new home for over sixteen years. I worked with the agency for five years, and I moved on to do personal styling for a high-end boutique. I was there for three years.

MOUNTAINS ARE THERE TO CLIMB

I now have another mountain to climb. I was diagnosed with DCIS, a form of breast cancer. The lump was removed. After having surgery, I needed radiation treatment for a while, and everything was all right for two years. I was clean with no signs of cancer. I was active and going to the gym. One day at the gym, I picked up a weight that I thought was a little too heavy, and I felt the strain. I went home, and I told my son. He said, "Mom, you will be okay. Just put some ice on it."

But it did not get better. I had my surgeon look. He thought it might be a hematoma and we would watch it. Several weeks went by, and it was around the time for my annual check-up. He looked at my breast and said the lump was still there. So, he sent me for an ultrasound. He did not like the report, and said, "I want to bring you into the hospital for a biopsy."

I had the surgery, and about two weeks later, he called me. I still remember the call and the conversation. After saying hello, he said, "Hi LaQue, how are you healing?" I said pretty good, then he said, "I have not so good news. I have to do a mastectomy."

I was in shock and said, "You are kidding me!"

He replied, "I wish I was."

I asked when.

He said, "Soon. The DCIS came back, and you cannot do radiation twice in the same area."

Talk about being thrown off my feet! I could not believe it. I was in shock. The boys were a great support. The son who moved out of state said, "Mom, I'll come home and take care of you." My youngest was with me as well. The fellow who was going to marry my daughter was there, and the young lady he married was a support as well.

The surgery and recovery went well. When it was time to see my chest, I asked one nurse to please stand with me as I looked into the mirror. When I looked at my chest, I was in shock. He removed one breast, and I was told it was going to be a long road to travel, with a lot of reconstruction.

There were about eight surgeries all together over the course of two years. But praise God. He brought me through a tough place again. As I continue to look ahead and not back, it was the most uncomfortable feeling I ever felt in my life. I could not lift, push, or pull anything for weeks. Months went by with me feeling out of touch with life as I knew it. Recovery was going well, but I was not up to going back to work. They held my position for three months and could not hold it any longer.

Through this healing process, my mind raced through all kinds of places, reflecting on the past, where I was going, and what I was going to do. What was my future? In conversation with a friend about my daughter and her father, I continued to tell a portion of my life, and the person said, "You should write a book."

A Sign

I love working with young girls and women. Teaching personal development workshops. Even when I taught at the modeling school, I remember the gratification from helping those students prepare for a quality of life, on how to build self-confidence and self-esteem.

Many of the girls had a lack of self-worth, and when some of them opened up to me, they told me things that hurt my heart. So, as I reflect on the lives I've touched, this helped me to bring my personal story to life.

As I looked back, I realized there were young girls and women going through the exact same things I have gone through. I had to count the cost and move forward for the lives that can benefit from my past. I want to help them create a bright future for themselves. As I reflect and think about the grief of losing my daughter, the thought of walking away from over 20-years of marriage, I was not in a good place.

Negative thoughts bombarded me. I had the feeling I did not want to live. My mother had passed away six months after my daughter. I felt very alone. My mind was racing, and I felt sorry for myself.

One day while in my bathroom, a light suddenly appeared, brighter than the light in my bathroom. I heard a still small voice, not out loud but enough that I knew it had to be the voice of God. He told me what would happen to the girls and women if I left this place and went to heaven. "There are lives that would be lost, and they are depending on you!"

THE PRESENCE IN THAT ROOM TRULY WAS A SUPERNATURAL EXPERIENCE. IT WAS AMAZING.

I will always remember it until the day I leave this earth. It has stuck with me, as if it just happened. My life flashed before me. All the things I was not proud of were brought to remembrance, and this voice wanted me to tell my story. It revealed there are women out here that are locked in a prison, with the same experiences, and they are afraid to expose the truth of what they are going through.

I cried uncontrollably. I could not stop. I became overheated, my whole body was affected. It was at that moment that I realized there was a purpose for me to live. A peace that I can't describe came over me, peace like I never felt before. That bright light faded away, and at that moment, I knew I had an encounter with God.

Months and years went by with me, never forgetting that experience. It was always with me. And even to this day. I now know that there is a perfect plan of God for my life. I am to help those who are victims of exploitation. Girls and women all over the world are being sold like a product for man's pleasure. I want to give insight as to why I'm working in this field.

I was recovering from my breast surgery, but in 2015, problems developed with the implant. Thank God it was only one breast that I lost with the mastectomy. The surgeon had to perform emergency surgery, remove the implant, and replace it with a new one. My blood levels were high, which meant there was an abnormality under the implant. The surgeon found out there had been bleeding, and he asked me if I had fallen. I said that I had not, but I was lifting weights, maybe too soon! But Glory to God, it went fine, and there was no cancer.

The surgeon cleaned it up and put a new implant in. It was like starting all over again. It has been three years of surgeries, but I'm moving forward with good health. I'm in physical therapy to gain strength and muscle tone. I'm so much stronger.

It's amazing how much strength you lose, having that much intervention. It takes a toll on the body and mind. It's a long process to get to a place of feeling like yourself again. I feel good and love the outcome of how my body is shaping up. The young man working with me is wonderful. During six months of physical therapy, when I felt a little down, he would not let me stay there. He would say, "LaQue, it will be a good day! Let's do this!" And we did. He always would say, "You got this!"

He has taken me to a place I never thought I would go. He helped me reach the level that I have obtained, lifting weights and getting strong. I am so grateful.

A Free Heart, And A
Free Soul, With A
Mind Renewed

While going through all this, another bomb was dropped on me. I found out a person whom I trusted, went to my sons to tell them that the money from my daughter's death was spent on drugs. One of my sons was most affected by this, and since then he only tolerates being around me. He really wants nothing to do with me.

This person reminded them of my past life. However, they failed to know that drugs were not my problem. My life in the past was broken, but drugs were not part of my struggle. After my daughter passed, I dealt with the broken marriage and the loss of my best friend, and my heart was broken into pieces. Turning to God was my refuge. Christmas and family time are not what it used to be. But these experiences have taught me to not give power to what hurts me. It is what it is. Only God can change hearts. I'm seeing life from where I've been victorious. The journey I've traveled and the life I survived is where few have lived to talk about it. Rejection is a milestone to what I have gone through. So, I rise from what is designed to break me. My mission is to help others get to this place. The thought is, you can be a victim, but you do not have to have a victim's mentality. Use rejection and the hurt in life as a steppingstone to VICTORY! I want you to know no matter what you go through, if it does not kill you, you can handle it.

Yes! I thought I would die. My heart was broken into pieces so many times, it's a wonder I did not die from a broken heart. But Glory to God, I'm still STANDING!

I've had people say hurtful things over the years.

"I could hate you."

"Let's ask Que. She knows about sex."

But these hurtful things remind me of something that was said in confidence.

"When you once were the victim, and you fight back and win, your enemy takes the stance of being the victim. So, he does everything in his or her power to bring you down."

By words, actions, or deeds, whatever they can use to hurt you, destroy your reputation, turn people against you and ruin friendships, that once were beautiful relationships! Words hurt. When those words attack you, you can't come back from the pain of hurting that person's heart with your mouth.

What has happened to me reminds me of what happened to Jesus Christ. He was despised and rejected by men. He was talked about for who his friends were, but he loved the lowly. The onlookers would belittle those who followed him. They shouted:

"You follow a man, who sits with thieves, and dines with whore mongers and prostitutes."

The 12 men who were with him in ministry all had a past.

JESUS MADE FRIENDS WITH THE PEOPLE THAT NO ONE WANTED TO BE AROUND.

He loved the sinner; he made them whole, and then he would say, "Pick up your cross and follow me and sin no more." When he accepted them and they him, he took their brokenness and healed them. They were made whole and then did ministry with Jesus. Mary the prostitute traveled with them along with his mother, whose name was also Mary. The women stayed with Jesus and his 12 disciples that worked ministry and traveled with them, healing the sick and setting the captive free. He did not reject anyone.

WHEN JESUS WENT TO THE CROSS AT THE TIME OF HIS DEATH, HE PLED:
"FATHER FORGIVE THEM FOR THEY KNOW NOT WHAT THEY DO!"
JESUS SAID, "THIS IS WHAT WE HAVE TO DO!"

I FORGIVE THEM ALL! EVERYONE WHO HAS HURT ME.

A forgiven heart is free. Forgive yourself and others, and choose not to walk in condemnation. Everyone Jesus chose as a disciple had a story, and he took them from a devastating place. He had no shame. He loved every one of them. There was no condemnation; the past was the past. They moved on to a better life. Study the New Testament, Matthew, Mark, Luke, and John and you will see they were not without sin.

In another story from the Old Testament, a man named Lot had a wife and family, and they were told to leave the city, "Run and don't look back." As they fled, Lot's wife disobeyed and looked back, and she turned into a pillar of salt. It is a detriment to look back. You won't turn into a literal pillar of salt, but you can become bitter and destroy your chance for freedom. Looking back can destroy you. You can't move forward to a new beginning if you are looking back at your old life. Wallowing in merciless self-pity is a grave, a box of self-containment.

You may think you don't have the power to forgive, but you do. You must forgive those who caused you pain. If you don't, you continue to give them power over your life. There are those living in the past 40 or 50 years or more, never forgiving, remembering the offense, the hurt, and distrust like it just happened.

STOP IT!
LIVE!
MOVE FROM THAT PLACE!

You may have children and grandchildren. If you don't let go, you pass un-forgiveness on to them. It becomes bondage and dysfunction.

Why forgive? It's for you more than for them. Forgiveness is to help you move forward in life, and not live life looking in the rearview mirror. When you don't forgive, it's like a cancer. It will eat away at your very being. It's hard. My flesh wants to tell them a few choice words and maybe a punch in the mouth.

To forgive it is not an easy task. Your mind, your heart, and soul fight. It hurts when you have been hurt to the core of your soul and heart. It is a war. I will not put myself in a place to be disrespected anymore. Sometimes you are blinded by the love you have for that person or persons, and you give them chances with hopes it will change. But people get comfortable disrespecting you. They take you for granted and continue to mistreat you in the form of disrespect and rejection.

Loving myself is something I had to learn. When you have been mistreated in the way I was, self-worth is the first thing to go. Once you get to a point where you can walk away from abuse and disrespect, that's called self-love. I learned that while going through the healing process, to love oneself is the best gift you can receive in life.

We will always have to go through many tests, and situations that we have no control over. Our job is not to let it affect us, and that is something we must work at every day. Whether we want it or not, there will always be something to test us. There is a saying: A person who can control his or her emotions is stronger than a man that can take a city.

Translation: when you control your response and not react in haste, you are the stronger one.

Keep your peace and do not allow anyone to push your buttons to make you act out of control. That is not to say we cannot be dissatisfied, and possibly angry. But power comes when we can control those emotions.

It has taken a long time for me to come to this reality and to use this tool every day. I find strength within my being, and it feels good.

WHO RAISED ME?

People make a choice to live a lifestyle. For some, it can be a dead end and for others a steppingstone. Some knowledge you cannot obtain unless you live it. You can use all that you learn and apply it to safeguard you, to make solid decisions, and to create a better life for yourself. You can share all that you have learned with others who may be heading in the wrong direction. Not everyone has a positive end. Some turn to drugs and it gets the best of them. Others are in the wrong place at the wrong time and suffer an early death. Young ladies get caught up with men who take advantage of them and do not have people who take an interest in them like I had.

It's amazing when I think about what and who I was involved with. It truly was divine intervention that I am here today to tell my story. There is only so much that I can put on paper to reveal the intensity of the exposure and what I went through as a young girl. There were people who wanted more for me. It was a life I could not imagine for myself, or even knew about as a young girl. The madams, the call girls, the strippers, the dancers–they all saw something in me. They called me a little sister because some had no family other than the people in the street. The older women would tell me, "You can be better than me." They all had a story. Some were so sad that there was no one to care for them other than a lying pimp.

I got to know and hear some of what they were going through. Some were homeless and had left home as young girl. Some of them got involved with a pimp who said, "I am your family." A common story was that they were thrust into this life with no choice. The older ones that knew better, did not fall for the lies. Surprisingly, a lot of them were well educated, but felt the life they were choosing was a solution for some things, such as taking care of child. Some were left with nothing, so they used their body as a business. Many do not realize this lifestyle devalues a human and can make someone feel they are at the point of no return and have lost all value. Self-esteem disappears, and you can feel lost. As time goes on, one can no longer have feelings about sex and intimacy.

The Italian family that took care of me had the people in the clubs afraid to talk to me. You may think that these kinds of people had no values. But that's not true. When we would talk, they would say "Que, go to school. Respect yourself, and demand respect from men. Don't allow them to use you."

The women I talked with would share their heartfelt feelings with me. One of them said to me, "I don't like this lifestyle. I want a husband and children, but it's too late for me. I am old and have been in this life a long time." The same woman then asked me, "What guy would want me?" At that moment, I felt a deep sadness, and it brought tears to my eyes. She looked at me and said, "You have a great future waiting for you, Que."

I am grateful to the women who educated me and saw there was more in life for me than what I was accepting. They saw a quality that could bring me to a successful life. They wanted me to have what they could not obtain for themselves: a career using my talent for business. They told me to value myself, and not let anyone use me. Being with them taught me lessons I could not learn from a book. I learned about personalities, character, self-lessness, and that love it is not sex. I now know what love really is!

My prayer and deepest desire is to bring healing and freedom to the reader of this book. What I thought to be the point of no return became a new life of wholeness, healing, and self-worth.

I know that there are those that have come into my life for me to touch and influence for the sole purpose of helping them find their way out of the places I've been or to prevent them from going there at all. I have been a mentor to so many young ladies that walked into my life. Some are in a place I once was, and they look to me for guidance to get out. Then there are those who made a change and are doing very well.

Unfortunately, some went back into that lifestyle. I shared my life, and I'm unashamed.

DON'T LET SHAME KEEP YOU FROM MOVING FORWARD

The past has a way of trying to rule your mind, bringing up old memories that try to stop you. It is a choice to make. You must choose to grow and heal from what life was to you. Choose to walk with your head up and shoulders back. You are developing confidence, self-esteem, knowing you have come through it all victoriously. This comes truly with the help of God, because I could not go through what I went through alone. It had to be Him, God. Dream your dreams and live them. Don't let the dead things get in the way. Yesterday is gone. Keep your eyes front and center. If you keep looking back, you can't see where you are going. You don't owe the world anything, but you owe it to yourself to live free and not be held captive by your past.

Life is a gift, and we don't know how long we can hold on to it. So, each day must have a meaning and a purpose. I don't want to take one day for granted, living life on purpose, and offering kind gestures to strangers, showing love to others, telling someone you love them, and meaning it.

When the anniversary of my daughter's death came, I reflected on who was with me, and how I felt when the police officer rang my doorbell. That was the hardest time of my life. It was hard to breathe. I remember every moment. She helped bring such joy into my heart. She was not only my daughter, but my friend. We would go to the movies, and she would say, "Okay, Mom. The movie is going to start. Are you going to talk?" I had a habit of talking just when the movie would start, and then she said, "Mom, the movie is on." We would laugh a lot. One day we went shopping together and then to dinner. On the way home after dinner while driving, I loosened the button on my slacks while in the car. When I got out of the car, my slacks fell to my knees. I forgot to refasten the button. My hands were full, and I could not grab my pants! She was laughing so hard and crying at the same time. She just stood there! I said, "Help me! Help me!" I was laughing myself. We were in a public parking lot. It was crazy funny! She had a great sense of humor. She is missed and is a great loss to me, but her love lives within me forever.

Love is an action word. I have told my children over the years the word is thrown around like you would say hello! It must come from the heart and then with action. I want to be able to fill a need when I see it!

I once saw a young mother who had no coat on, and her two young children had no winter coats as well. It was eleven degrees outside. We had a snowstorm the day before. I let her walk in front of me to get the children into her car, and I wished I had $250.00 or more to give her and say, "Go get the children winter coats and one for yourself." I do not want to walk away from that need.

I hope and pray my life story has blessed you in some way. I hope it will encourage you to know that life is about lessons, regardless of what life gives you. You may endure the loss of what you cared about, and people who you would have never thought could walk away from you when you needed them the most. It can be heartbreaking, but you go through life's lessons, and yes, they are lessons. I have learned from every one of them. It's a lesson because I have taken what was thrown at me to use it as a steppingstone to improve and become stronger, and not give up. This was told to me a long time ago by the Italian Mafia family that took me under their wings.

You are smart.

You are beautiful.

You can be whatever you want to be. Go to school.

Go out with guys your own age.

These words told me that I can be someone. And the words did not come from the people who should have been the ones to encourage me. It all came from the outside. I am grateful to the men who took nothing from me. These men will forever be in my heart.

I want to tell you that I know there was divine intervention in my life. Where I came from, there is no way I should be alive today. It was me and God. I know that now. There was evil in the world then, like there is now. The glory goes to God for using the people who saved my life from death and destruction, and now I can help someone else. I had to learn forgiveness for myself and my abusers. It was not easy, but I found power in forgiveness. I took God as my Father because I had no real father to protect me. God loved the world to send Jesus Christ to save that which was lost, and that is true love. I can go and sit at his feet in prayer. I accepted Jesus Christ as my Lord and Savior. It was the only thing I found that had substance, meaning, and purpose.

Things Are Not As They Seem - Do Not Judge

How can you say you love your sister and brother, and fail to show them love when they have fallen? During the time of Christ's ministry, there was a woman who was sleeping around and the people in the town found out and planned to stone her. Jesus found her in her state and chastised those who sought to punish her. Jesus shouted, "He who is without sin, let him cast the first stone." No one responded, and they left. Jesus said to the woman, "They condemn you not, and neither do I. Go and sin no more."

How do you know the pain if you have not felt it? You can read about it, hear people talk about it, and teach on it. There are many who are exploited and used beyond imagination. There are young children thrust into a sick adult world. There are young girls who will never feel like a little girl, ever. They will live the rest of their life in fear, reliving the torment of what has happened.

But, through the grace of God, women like me who have been there can walk through the healing process. They will feel the love and understanding. With the help of others, they can know that we also have been in that very place, and they can gain self-worth and self-esteem. We can mend and heal. With help, they will no longer be broken but gain wholeness. They, too, can have this testimony of victory!

When you read the life of Jesus, he loved the people who were in a bad place in life. He spent time with all people, like the people I have spoken of and the life I lived. We cannot think of ourselves as better than the person who is lost. You don't know what the story is. They could be a child who was taken advantage of sexually and exploited. It's easy for a young girl to turn to prostitution. She has lost her self-worth. When used that way, some will turn to drugs to dull the pain and the memory of the horror of that life. And then some don't want to live anymore, so suicide becomes a way out. But there is light at the end of the tunnel. Women like me have found the way out.

START * PASS * THROUGH

There is a beginning. Travel forward through to the end. It's a place you will never pass through again. Why let your heart and soul live there? The people responsible for your pain and hardship are dead within themselves in that self-made grave. When you refuse to let go, and refuse to release them with forgiveness, they continue to have power over your life, and keep you locked up within yourself. It's harsh, but if you don't let go of the hurt and the pain of it all, that's where you will live. Don't let what happened to you dictate your way of life. When you are a victim of abuse, you are stripped of any feelings of self-worth and love of yourself. In that state of mind, it is hard to love others. It's about letting the love of God break the chains and shackles. The hardship and loss will dissipate, and you can forgive yourself and forgive others.

I thank God I'm healthy and strong. My thought is you can be a victim but not live like one! When you have been hurt like this, you can't let your heart become cold. You will learn everyone is not out to hurt you. Trust does not come easy and sometimes you must take baby steps, and make certain the one you open your heart to is worthy of you letting them in. Don't be afraid to love; it's a great feeling to love others. You can still guard yourself and use wisdom when you let someone into your personal space. There are so many people who are too guarded, and they have a fractured personality. They are not nice to be around. When you start to love yourself, you will find that you live in a fishbowl, meaning what you see is what you get. You have self-confidence and self-esteem, so you don't care about pleasing people. Yes, you want to be liked and accepted, but that's not what you are living for. We must be kind to others and be a nice person, then we become likable.

Everyone loves a nice person, so you must like and love yourself. Then liking and loving other people will come easy. Look to the heart of a person. How are they? Because when a person speaks, it comes from the heart. If they spew out trash and ugliness, that's coming from the heart. If there is bitterness, it truly will show itself. It seems like they have pickle juice in the morning for breakfast. There will always be someone or something that will try to get in the way of us moving forward in life. It's a battle to strive for success. Anything worthwhile is worth fighting for, no matter what it is.

I'm not only writing to you, but it's also a reminder of my personal goal for myself. I'm starting a new chapter in my life. I've lost a lot in life, but I am grateful for what I have left. There are those who love me and that means a lot. I can't change the ones who don't, or the ones who walked away. I have accepted the things I cannot change. I ask God for the courage to change the things I can, and the wisdom to know the difference. That is my day-to-day promise to myself, to move forward, look at the results and not the journey. I need to keep my eyes on where I'm going, no matter how rough the road. Yes, there are bumps and not always a smooth path. I think about what I want for myself at this time in my life. I am not bitter and would like to share my life with a wonderful man to be my husband, who will love me the way God intended a man to love a woman! There are women I have spoken with who feel bitter and made up their mind not to marry ever again. To me, that is giving that past relationship that did not work out the power to affect what could be a beautiful union of a man and woman. So, I have a dream of having a new life filled with true love and happiness. That is my hope for all who have been in a place of brokenness loss and abuse.

There is another chapter. It's not the end of your story. Every man does not have an agenda to be abusive or to cause harm. When you've traveled through the hard places of life, you should become smarter, and wisdom becomes your teacher. We must step out and try again. We must open ourselves up to receive the beautiful things life has to offer when they come.

You can rise above it and not live in a victim's mentality. There are many who live there and feel the world owes them something, and angry at everyone. I made up my mind not to be that person. And by the grace of God, don't you live there. Take what you have learned from me sharing my heart and soul with you and be free.

Build Strong Relationships

You may be in a relationship that is not worthy of you.

If your partner is physically or mentally abusing you, they are not the one. That is not true love. It's not love at all. I've been in some relationships where the person hit me, choked me, and then made me have sex with him. That is sick!

I had another relationship where he and I had a disagreement. He moved toward me like he was going to hit me, and I shouted, "WHAT!" Then he pushed me in the chest. I pushed him back, and he grabbed my chest. I grabbed a broom, and I hit him with that broom. He got the broom away from me and hit me with it. I kicked him, aiming for his private parts. He threw the broom down and grabbed my leg, twisting my foot. I fell to the floor, hard. I felt lightheaded, almost unconscious. I said in a low voice, "Call 911." The fire department came, and I remember asking, "What's wrong with my leg?" I lifted my head, trying to look down at my foot. One man said your foot is broken. I could see it was twisted around, and the medic said he was going to take care of me.

They put it into this bubble kind of thing, so it could not

move. I found out it was dislocated and broken. I was taken to the emergency room, and they gave me something for the pain while waiting for the orthopedic surgeon to come. He was the one who had to put my foot back together. I stayed in the hospital for ten days, and I had to learn to walk again on that foot. They had to put screws in the ankle, and a plate with screws down the side of my lower leg. For months I had to regain mobility, using a wheel-chair, walker, crutches, then a cane. There was a lot of physical therapy.

To be completely transparent and truthful, I noticed a few deep scratches on my abuser's face. I put up a good fight.

Some of you are in a relationship that has been like this, or shows signs of this very thing. Get out of it! It could have been worse for me. The surgeon thought I would walk with a limp, but glory to God, I don't. Full healing. It's not as strong as it was, but anything that was broken is never like it once was. It is like a used car. It runs great, but it's not brand new.

For some of you that are in an unhealthy relationship, don't look away from the signs. Don't let him break something on you, or in you. You become broken inside when you stay in a situation, knowing there is something wrong. It's not a bad thing to be alone until the right one comes. When you learn to value yourself, you will wait. I have decided to wait until the right one comes into my life. You tell your body why you are waiting. Don't give your body to everyone who wants it. Save it for the one who is worthy of having you. Love yourself, even when you don't feel love from others. You may go through rejection, but don't let that effect you loving you. Forgive yourself. It's not your fault even if you have been told it was, or you think it was.

Forgive the person or people who took advantage of you–the ones who hurt you. You may say, how can I do that? It was painful. YOU CAN! If you don't, you give them power over you, meaning the things they did to you will continue in your mind, heart, and soul. That's why! IT'S NOT EASY. You must do this for your freedom. You don't want to become that bitter person that no one would like to be around. When you take your power back, they can no longer control you because you decided to make this choice. I've made a choice for it not to affect me anymore. It took time because it hurt my heart. But I no longer carry the pain I once felt. I know a lot of you are carrying the pain of someone very close to you that has caused heartfelt pain, but it can be done. You must forgive them.

MY PRAYER IS THAT MY LIFE STORY WILL HELP ALL WHO READ THIS BOOK.

BROKEN TO WHOLENESS.

Pitiful or powerful! Triumphant through the dark valley of life, your tragedies can be a steppingstone to victory!

Insight On Those Who Don't Forgive You!

I 've spoken of forgiving ourselves and others, but not about those who have not forgiven you! Some reasons may include a breakup, something you did or did not do, or was something that you were expected to do. There are people who take on another person's grievances, as though it was against them. Maybe they don't like you, for whatever reason. It could be jealousy. You're good looking, you have a great personality, and you have boldness. People can dislike you because of what you represent. Someone may like you or love you more than that person who is showing resentment towards you. You may show them who they are or not. You could be a reminder of who they would like to be. So, jealousy is the factor of it all. Their own insecurities show up, and they sometimes do something to sabotage a potential friendship. They will make up untrue things about you. There will always be a LOOSE LIPS FREDDIE and FORK TONGUE SUSIE. Freddie can't hold water; he always has something to say about someone that is negative. Susie will speak nice things to your face, but behind your back, she curses you.

Out of the blue, Charlie showed up. Charlie was someone who I thought was in a good place after breaking up many years prior. He asked if he could visit me, and I said sure.

While having conversations about past events in our relationship, his words were unexpected. He wanted to clear the air about some thoughts he was having.

"Why did you fall out of love with me?"

Accusations poured out to me, including things I did and did not do. Finally, I took the high road, and said, "If I hurt you, I'm sorry. I will ask you to tell my boys the truth about what you know to be true about me and the financial hardship I was going through. It was no fault of my own." I pled to the one who harbored bitterness toward me.

He replied, "IT WILL NEVER HAPPEN!"

Needless to say, I was shocked. It was hard for me to accept that this person could change the broken relationship between a mother and her son, but chose not to. He did it for revenge. There was nothing left to be said, so I closed the door to that situation.

There will be haters. Don't let anyone put you back in prison. I have learned through this journey that if someone wants to walk away, open the door.

People who are not free don't want to see others free from anything that has been bondage of any kind.

There will be someone or something to try to make you stumble. Don't believe the lies or voices in your head. Don't believe the people who want you to fail. Believe in yourself. You can be victorious and not a victim!

I am moving on, and you should, too. When our enemy sees that we can move on, and not stay wounded from the evil done to us, we win. Now they are the defeated. Our job is to keep focusing on our journey with the expectation of making it to our destination. Dream your dreams and only share them with other dreamers.

Not everyone will support you, encourage you to move forward, or to take chances.

Don't waste time on unfruitful relationships. Clean house. Remove those who have no intention of doing anything for themselves. Remove those that have no encouragement for you. You don't need them around, it's like they pour ice water on your fire. We can't let anyone dim our light.

The whispers of that person who wanted revenge have influenced family members. I don't try to fix people or situations anymore. That is God's job. It's the love. I fill my heart with peace, and I walk in love with all people. We cannot make a person like or love us. If they don't, we have to accept their decision and move on. We can surround ourselves with people who want to be around us and not just tolerate us.

Father God knows how to fix what is broken. Our job is to be still and let Him take care of it. Do not let go of the peace in our own hearts!

WHERE I AM TODAY

I am healthy.

There was a time when I could not push or pull, and could not lift a gallon of water. Today I have a person to encourage me to do more. My physical therapist, who worked with me from the beginning of my recovery from breast cancer, encourages me. I will finish strong.

I work at eating healthy and clean. I avoid preservatives if possible. I include dark greens and lots of fruit in my diet. I love yogurt with nuts and raisins, and I drink plenty of water. Hydration is so important. I can eat watermelon every day, and sometimes I do. I love Italian food, and don't forget the Italian cookies! A low-fat frozen yogurt is never refused. I snack on fresh carrots, cucumber, and celery sticks with a homemade dressing that I dip them in.

What are my plans from here? I feel my future is bright. I am a mentor to young professionals; I will continue with that commitment. It is a great program. I will also tell my story to whoever will listen, including schools, colleges, group homes, churches, and youth centers. My dream is to provide a home for girls and women who have no family and are working toward a new life. With the skills and training I have obtained over many years, I will help them to gain a profession and prepare them for a reputable job. I would like to share my story not just with women and girls in the United States, but with those in other countries.

If you think no one loves you, you're wrong.

I DO!

I have shared my story with you for the sole purpose of helping you have a successful life. My hope is that my past can help save your future. My prayer is that you will be blessed and one day you will be able to help someone with your own story!

La'Que Duren

Uplifting Posts
During My Journey

I would like to share some posts I have written while going through my own personal struggles. And I decided to share them with others, and now you, with hopes it will strengthen you.

June 2016

Your past does not define your future or who you can become. Your self-worth is not based on people's opinion or approval of you. What defines you is loving yourself. Know God loves you unconditionally, don't regret the journey you have traveled and the storms you went through. Only look back to see how far you've come. The road you traveled can help someone find their way!

November 2016

A HEART THAT KNOWS!
When I think about the beginning of life. The heart is the

first thing that is detected, even before the full development of the body. As time goes on, it takes on the full meaning of life, happy, sad, hate, love. Then one day, you look, and you see you no longer know life as you once knew it, and then a loss of a loved one that was a part of your everyday existence. The heart that beat with the joy of knowing has broken into many fragments, and you can't find the connection to rebuild. Each breath is hard to take. There are no words to make you feel better. But there is a man who created that heart. The developer knows the structure and how to rebuild the foundation, so it's up and running again. That man is, GOD JEHOVAH, and His son JESUS CHRIST. One day you see the light shining and you can feel your heart beating normally again; the pain has let up, and then feeling comes back into your being. Then you live life again, knowing the one that left just changed their address and you will one day be together again! So, we must see them in our everyday, living, and celebrate who they were, and keep them alive! The things you know they like to do. Love, sing, dance, embrace one another, have fun times with family, and meaningful friendships!

November 2017

THE HEALING HEART!
Shh....... Take your rest now! The comforter has come. God Said. "Be still and know that I am God." Quiet moments, control, and hear your breathing, layout flat to relax, a long shower, asking the Master to let the rain of his presence fall. Sleep in the clothes you were born in. There is something to sleep freely while going through a healing process. Take a rest every day, a bathroom break, to be quiet. Step away from the noise. There are times you may visit the valley of grief; you just pass through. There is some pain while healing, but the process has started. You start to notice

beauty that you never took the time to see God's handiwork. Now you become grateful. The dawn of a new day! You notice the sparrows flocking around, playing with each other. Emotions try to come into anger. Then love forces out that feeling of anger; it only creates more pain. It's when we go to the quiet place with the Comforter that he won't let this heart become cold and harden. Love floods the soul, and resentment has no place here! It's only Him, the Creator, that this heart is a heart of flesh. It's filled with peace and the overflowing love of God!

April 2018

Just a reminder to all who may be going through a hard time. I love to reflect and remind myself of why I'm here; we all have a purpose, and what does not kill us will make us stronger. Our life experiences can encourage, strengthen and give hope. You may be thinking you cannot move forward to a new beginning, but you can. Life Is so worth living when you see the fruit of helping another person who benefited from what you came through yourself. I hope this will encourage you!

ACKNOWLEDGMENTS

I GIVE GLORY AND HONOR
TO THE ONE WHO FIRST LOVED ME.
GOD JEHOVAH AND HIS SON JESUS CHRIST
MY LORD GOD USED THE JOURNEY I WAS ON TO
GIVE ME A PURPOSE!

I am grateful for the gift of motherhood; there is nothing to compare to the honor of being a caregiver to a human being, given to me by God, Our Creator. I have been blessed to give birth to four wonderful children, who gave me a new life so worthwhile.

I have been adopted by one son from a different mother, which makes me a mother of five, four sons and my daughter, as well as being a mentor to many others.

Recently I had an emergency visit to my hospital facility. I thank the first responders who came to my rescue, and the medical team who took great care of me. Thank you to the technician, who would not stop until she got a clear view of my heart. I'm grateful to Neem, who kept me on the phone until the fire department came, then rushed to the ER to be by my side. Mir, you tracked me down until they got a phone to me, to see if I was all right. Thank you for spending the rest of the day with me until all tests were done. Grateful to God for the good report! You took me to a wonderful brunch after I was discharged. Thank you both for your unconditional love and respect. You lifted me up when the funds were low.

Pastor Johnathan Verna and Pastor Tom, thank you for your support. God used you and your ministering gifts to help me get through the death of my daughter.

I'm grateful for family and the time spent with my grand-daughters over the years. I have a recent addition, a daughter from a different mother who has joined her life with my son, and there is one.

I was invited to go hiking with some family members and I was told it's no big deal. Guess what it was! As we get close to where we needed to be in the woods, it turned into rock climbing, ten feet high or more. I heard, "Come on. You can make it!" Needless to say, I was stretched. I was grateful for the strength I received during physical therapy. My therapist, David, who pushed me beyond what I thought to be my limit. Do I want to go hiking again? Yes. Rock climbing? No.

To Stephanie, thank you for cheering me on all these years. Hank, thank you for your gift of kindness.

I am grateful to my brother, who recently went to heaven. Just before leaving this earth, he said, "Did you write that book?" I answered that it was not finished yet. He raised his voice and said, "Well, get to it!"

Thank you to my sister-in-law, Carole, who has been inspirational.

Thank you to all who have inspired me to take this journey. To my family, the ones who are here, and the ones who have gone. My brother-in-law, Richie, my sister Joanne, who has been there from the very beginning. Thank you to my few true friends, in the full meaning of that word. Jo, my hair stylist and friend, who traveled a great distance so I could look my best for my son's wedding. Thank you, Tricia, who I can truly call a friend; you were there while I was recovering from surgery.

If we can say we have one or two real friends, we should count ourselves wealthy. Thinking of friendships and family, apart from God, that is everything. We must love each other, not just say it! Our actions speak louder than words. To my family, we have wonderful memories to hold on to. We must live life on purpose, enjoy every day and celebrate one another. The life we have is a gift given by God!

About the Author

LaQue Duren was born in Boston, Massachusetts. She is a mother of four and has three granddaughters. Her hobbies include acting, working out at the gym, traveling, and dancing.

LaQue attended Northeastern University in Boston and applied herself to business courses. She later received a degree in makeup application at Charles Revson of New York, which made her qualified to instruct others in makeup consultation and application techniques.

Furthering her education in fashion and modeling, LaQue went to several industries and received a degree, which allowed her to teach modeling and personal development. LaQue then became the owner and manager of a fashion hair and makeup boutique. She has had professional training with the girls Coalition of Boston on how to prevent teen prostitution and exploitation of girls. LaQue has worked with teen mothers' programs and with women in prison. She has been involved in various outreach programs, traveled statewide working with colleges, vocational schools, and high schools along with teaching at various career centers.

LaQue is a motivational speaker that is charismatic when she speaks and leaves an impression on the audiences both large and small.

facebook.com/laque.duren

linkedin.com/in/laqueduren

CPSIA information can be obtained
at www.ICGtesting.com
Printed in the USA
BVHW042019110122
626006BV00009B/62